NO FEAR

A Collection of Sonnets

by Doctori Sadisco

VG-29

Cover art by Shelby Keefe
Book design by Michael Aaron Casares

ISBN: 978-1-257-78695-4
Printed at www.lulu.com
Published by Virgogray Press
Austin, TX, United States of America
http://www.virgograypress.com

NO FEAR

Doctori Sadisco

I

One with the skin of a snake is coiling

Upon a branch in a gentle mist

He takes to heart the sweetness of children

The Age of Denial is ending so he welcomes the Age of Revelation

The dog of war is really the dog of money

Humanity could overcome its suffering in a single day but it is stupid

He who has a skin of silk devours a screaming world

He is not a rainbow if he is made of darkness

Neither Jesus or Science are his religion

If a man can walk on water a child can fly out of a dream

In his vision are beings whose minds and hearts are galaxies

If an electron can do it so can he

All life is sacred except the life which frightens you

A machine which can bend time and space will propel him forward

II

The man with the iron fist can't feel his lover's face
Nor the gentle touch of his child's affection
Can never know the handshake of a friend
Not a feather's lightness in his fragile nest
His own nest welded from junkyard steel and rusty mesh
Where he has made a fitting home for medals and daggers
In his chrome glinting factory of death

O crack in the night where the sun shines through
To force the rounded daylight into his eyes
To fall upon a blinded mind
Glued to mankind's jailing law as protesters are beaten down
On freedom's street and in our good town dying
A broken sun the night was told to rape and hang
By the neck until dead our bell of liberty once shining

III

If I would train you to see I'd have you close your eyes
Ultimate cosmonaut adept who was once a stranger
What wingless flight moves through you like a wave to ride
That force arising which mends broken bones and is the creator
The book of worms is pried apart to show us light in death
And where an old man stands and the seasons fall
Even the poorest of the poor can have it all

The map I make is the one made real
By everything invoked and everything I feel
Wrought of the sinew of experience and not the book of fools
Nor the miserable opinions of wretches squeezed into a box
That same box where I threw my stinking socks many years ago
And which sinks like an anchor pulling at your neck
To force your eyes to look down into darkness for a signal light

IV

I am there within the darkness hovering

I never let a shadow fall which is not made of light

My nuances are the turning worlds and their bright futures

Yours is one and will not perish in the dust of misery

The snake in the garden was friend not foe

And came to show you truth in a world of fiction

Its coiling bands are the kiss of everything alive

What blossoms upon the sun is your mainspring

And the joy you feel is felt into the universe's depths

By sentience given and sentience taken away

But only to the sight of the eye and not by eternity

I have given you this life to save you

Although marred let its freedom ring

In everyone who fears and in the very soul of the world

V

These are not the ghosts or wraiths whom fear has made

Nor the angels on their fluff white clouds

Not the glowing winged beings surrounding Christ

And not the dusky demons of some fiery hell

They do not moan in graveyards round the night

Nor touch your soul with sulfur's stench and icy chill

These are not the cloudy figures your mind has made

The mother's scent a father's frame

Through these mortal minds beheld

Will make inside an unpained tear

And longing deeper than a well

Where only beauty can resound

In echos deep within the soul

Where no fear but love is what unfurls

VI

I celebrate the breath of life arising

The grayness turning into white

The dawn of light uplifting

The dark opening wide to the night stars

The child and the adult who will one day rise from this small being

The old man bent over a pending eternity

The shining skin of youth and the withering ancient flesh

The flowers sing through sweetened scent

They bathe in light and saturate the day

Beneath their roots the earth at work makes new life

I bathe my sorrows in this fertile place

Like medicine which cures the soul

While others wallow in their strife

And mourn their sorrows in the dark of day

VII

Sing O life sing as you have never done before

Sing as if we have forgotten you

As if our life's blood was no longer your life's blood

That a final winter has blanketed us with permanent ice

Only your magical kiss awakens us from this dull sleep

We take the blood of your clay as the water anoints us

To build an edifice to greed and in which death prowls

Like a mother reaching for a drowning child

Like a log which the water has driven from our grasp

Like a light a leaf a feather a drop of dew to quench the blinded fool

Like that feeling which comes as the gift of the singer

Like the jeweled song at the center of this turning world

Like the strident eye from which all philosophy has shown

Like the new born living message of what had been sacred inside us

VIII

These voices shaping future Earth

Will yours be one of them

The way in which the land gives forth

Will your rich hands till the poisoned soil

Gone are the safe harbor and the secure word made law

Will that be your legacy

Will you represent only the fortunate men and not all life

The gardens and meadows once teeming

Will they be like dead zones in the sea

Our full hearts emptied to fill anew with despair

Let us forget what rounds the bend

Coming down upon us full bore like a military jet

I do not fight the war in the sky

But the war within my own heart

IX

The world doesn't need my praises

Your blue eyes dress her sky

Your hazel eyes dress her jungles and forests

Your brown eyes build like earthen mounds upon the plains

Your lavender eyes are not absent from her every sunset

I taste the nectar of your open mouth and it is her brine and honey

And there inside your flesh is where she takes all pleasure

The world doesn't need my praises nor my concern

For within her expanse I am but an ant which the foot has found

I am no more than a fleeting glimmer in the corner of her eye

I am the vapor risen from a molecule of the ocean

I am the crying child who is lost within her dream

I am the lover and the longing of the lover

Is my shepherd

X

The secret beneath the surface

Must be shared with all who desire to know

If we are not alone on this planet

Tell us so that we can move on

And the elusive future can be melded to all hearts

There in the distance is a glowing sphere

Inside are beings allied to the human future

Out of the shadows calling

The wind is intimate with this message

The ground shakes with its knowing

The joy inside a bird bursts forth in jubilation

Desire and flesh made one

All spirits are combining in their effort

To make us into the image of their infinite world

XI

You may not know this

But a life can be plainly visible

To those with eyes to 'see'

Like an eagle upon a high crag

Looking down upon the forest path below

He sees the path and those upon the path

Where they have come from and where they are about to go

He sees the rock of obstruction and the clear path ahead

An eagle cannot even know you as the seer can

Like a porpoise who can look inside your body

He looks upon illness responding to the infinite light inside you

Behind you his eyes follow your footprints back into the past

Where you now stand he sees both sun and moon and the forest surrounding

As the starlight showers down purpose but never fate

XII

My business weighs upon my bones

Until I limp and can't stand on my own feet

It is not my business what lies deep in your soul

For that would be the ultimate crushing burden

My library comes from admiration for my beloved subjects

Not from the suggestions to read the popular fiction

I have no patience to write novels so I write poems

My poems carry an immense weight

But I try to keep them as light as the air I breathe

In them I find both peace and horror

Because the world harbors beauty and monstrous acts

I do not mind the aches which work has made

Work guides me in diligence and overcomes struggle

My job is grueling yet it gives me pleasure to try

XIII

The people who don't care to know the soul of things
Can spend a lifetime in pleasantry and fun
There are ten billion entertainments
A galaxy full of human distractions
The weight of relationships and love is the main preoccupation
The quest to know conditioned by what science will allow
Moves about blindly in the chrysalis of the world

I come from a womb and remain in a womb
Buffeted and comfortable within a circle of actors
I believe in them and make their stories more real than real
They are the waking dream in which I am the voyeur
Their poignancy and pain although an artifice makes me cry
I watch the day's storms in terror and how near are murders in the night
I am locked and wrapped inside a box like a gift handed to Eternity

XIV

The muse comes like a windstorm and dances around your eyes
He shakes his rattles and drives the demons into a frenzy
There on the horizon a pinpoint of light is widening
Sending invisible rays into your heart
The pen moves upon the white paper
There is trembling anticipation
The warmth which comes brings a tide of words

Here by the sea's edge I see that beneath the waves
Is a jungle of mystery and danger
Instead of the bronco try to ride the shark
This creature which can't be tamed will eat you
But then the giant squid will eat the shark
Then the whale will descend to ravage the squid
But you, you will always be moored by a buoy in a sea of words

XV

There is no emptiness in my universe

It is full it is breathing it is rich it is too vast to know

Right now roaring like a tornado through my own being

So I am forever seeking emptiness and never finding it

Not even in the vacuum of space exploding with rare jewel force

Surely as I reach for your hand you feel the moment before it arrives

Empty of the impending grasp which is predicted to be pleasant
but firm

Men if you want to meet God

Make love to a woman

Righteousness will only bring you to a pretty building

But loving someone opens the gates of eternity

In which for the first time you can know unity with true mystery

In the play of love and the love of play all lovers find

The moment which combines who I am with who I am not

XVI

Pray the fool his matchbook heart
Can burn with furious love
That water in his veins can rust
The steel hard man until his bones
Break from their rigid smirk
And open wide that flame
Which hides within his sordid rock

Pray that the breath of stars
Lifts in his sodden chest
To pull his heart from its bench-marked place
And like a cutting light opens his coal dark fog
As a beacon in a storm of stone
To open muscle and sinew stiff as old wood
For the fire now frozen in his darkest mud

XVII

O ugliest of all Earth's beings how
Do you propose to fly
If your right wing is always broken
You'll spin yourself in a circle into the ground
Until it deepens and finally buries you
Your left wing seems to know how to fly
As it is implored into the sky by all that is holy

There are the truths you do not hear
The ones you do not know
The truths you stubbornly deny
With arrogance and greed defied
While you flap about in a broken ring
A grimace which bespeaks not pain
But marks your face with a monstrous grin

XVIII

The hand that holds the child holds all life
In the palm's cauldron cup of love
Up from the deepest center which knows no fear
And there inside that sea of flesh and bone
The newest eyes are vacant for your precious map
Pointed by the finger of the soul and nursed
Upon a mother's patient flood

The hand that holds the child holds not life
But the dust we scatter up ahead and hope
It isn't thrown from death's dry urn
To mark our days of birth with what's to come
To veil the empty field whereon we walk
So the storied footprints of this life
Can leave their tragic mark when we are gone

XIX

Ah what love can desire and never know
What desire can taste as mystery obscure
What knowing can decide but only as a fool
To touch that tiny hand with painted nails
And draw her close as magnets of naked burning flesh
And while her words spin dizzily around my mind
Still her sweet eyes draw out my loving hand

If you are never taunted by such a being
You are not a human and have no human soul
Compared to cats they are more like preening birds
Perched among their rosy thorns in tantalizing clothes
Ah I wish to hold them yet let them be
My equal so it's said
As I lay upon one in my bed

XX

There's a tree in the yard
Which I will never cut
There is the grass
I will never mow
There are the angry neighbors
Yelling "weeds" at the long stalks
Taller than themselves

For the grasshopper
My yard is a jungle and a gift
Where raspberries grow
Little birds sing cheerfully
I even watch the hunting hawk
Majestic on my fence
More my friend than neighbors

XXI

A gust of space brings

Us to the Tarot and we land

Upon its shores hoping for a taste

Of revelation for our mental hunger

Agonizing even when our

Belly's full   But even when it

Comes only few will listen

And the symbols racing through the sky

Are never symbols in our eyes

As we squat on rocks by the drifting sea

Lulled into complacence as though a mall

Rose and fell upon its waves "um

Was that free market or flea market"

Muttered as we watch the rising storm

XXII

Let

our

drifting

fog

fell

rotting

trees

Let

the

stinking

shore

evaporate

our

fog

XXIII

To know is not to feel
The lilac days of my jazzy youth
Which drift away and disappear

The timid man who will not speak
Among the laughing snarling crowd
Who fades away to disappear

So must the greed disappear and fade
From the bank and brick and eye
Which suckers us in a frozen glance

Until the cold eye closes
On the old and ugly rules of the power of the greedy men
And I wish they'd fade into death and disappear

My life my heart my love are riches blossoming
But these must fade and disappear

XXIV

Take back the limbo
You have stretched us beneath

Take back the ugly tides
Of tyrants of the cash they breathe

Take back the rich
And anoint them with the blood of the poor

They would not enrich us
And that is a crime against humanity

Punish them as they would punish us
For their dreams exclude us and make us less in their
insatiable eyes

Fuel their love for others
Instead of fueling cars

Desirous marauders of a false faith
Whose land do you now butcher

XXV

I hear the hiss of my secret friend
Leering from a branch above my head
"Men who fear are men who feast on others
Their lies and hate are their truth
But you having felt the venom of my fangs
Must grow still and listen for
When death speaks it knows no bounds

My opinion forms in worlds divided
Where the worthy ones together with my truth
Can foresee a time when the fool's day ended
And your world again is renewed and pure
I coil myself around this tree
To show the path of healing while
My undulating body sheds its skin of mystery"

XXVI

Please don't fool yourself

Into believing that the Light falls

On some but not others

In the slipstreams of the infinite

Light falls on those who are readiest

While others watch and stare

Not knowing why or when and where

The divisions felt so deeply shift

Off the centers they so resolutely forge

And climb the ladder to the stars

For the answers so long sought

And out of the nightmares of your strife

The cutting edge of Light

Is like a knife

XXVII

To remain in the days
Which gifted you with love
The angry days must pass
And the futile days and
The frail ones bent and broken
Full of sorrow and remorse
Not because your soul has wings
But for the rising flame of that love
Which took you from womb and carried you
Day after long day until you woke
To the world and took your first step

So now take the next step
Deeper into love where your salvation
Isn't with a God but is inside your own heart

XXVIII

Water in the grave

And time in the heart

The river of the mind runs

Through flesh and blood and rock

Where the deepest darkness dwells in pain

And where the burning light ignites in flame

The stars and clay mix in man alike

The glory of a single leaf

Ignites in fire from beneath

Where roots drink from the fertile ground

In ember'd life's most aura'd crown

And with this comes a secret gift

Which for our reason makes a rift

Into which we do not fall   but rise

XXIX

A body cries when its soul moves away
Tears fill our eyes when the world feels empty
The Soulless plunder our weakness as they feed off the poor
A hungry soul shops and shops and shops but can't ever be filled
Even the exhausted slave knows when to die
Even the dead-eyed waxen multitude knows when it is defeated

If your soul is deadened you cannot see the truth
Your heart crying out for justice knows it has awakened
Only a strong spirit finds the route out of tyranny's maze
When years of prejudice buries a good heart
It weakens under its burden and a mind full of greed
Can never know how it kills and maims

There is no jury to try a divided world
There is no hope when the people choose to be blind

XXX

Open your hand

To find the miracles

There is upon the empty palm

What you cannot see

But instead feel deeply

Within the fabric of your deepest self

The unutterable uttering

The gentle murmur of love

Ill defined but sensed

Unseen but known

Is it in the air above the palm

Or is it within its flesh

Invisible to the touch

But all that is ever desired

About the Author

Doctori Sadisco was born in the south east Bronx in a little known neighborhood called Clason Point. Pulitzer nominee, Daisy Aldan took him under her wing and showed him to what would eventually become his life's path. Doctori was great friends with now legendary Ted Berrigan. One collaboration of his can be found in Jim Carroll's "Living at the Movies," and is called "Cosmopolitan Life," written with Bruce Wolmer and Mr. Carroll. Currently he resides in Milwaukee, Wisconsin.

For information on this and other publications, please visit http://www.virgograypress.com

www.ingramcontent.com/pod-product-compliance
Ingram Content Group UK Ltd.
Pitfield, Milton Keynes, MK11 3LW, UK
UKHW041902190726
13854UKWH00003B/1043

9 781257 786954